THE G.I. SERIES

Matthew Brady photographed Major Robert Anderson, the 'hero of Fort Sumter' holding an 1860s forage cap and wearing the 1851-pattern dark blue cloak coat for officers with three black silk galloons between the elbow and cuff to designate rank. Anderson's double-breasted 1851-pattern frock coat as prescribed for field grade officers is evident underneath the coat. (RGB)

THE G. I. SERIES

THE ILLUSTRATED HISTORY OF THE AMERICAN
SOLDIER, HIS UNIFORM AND HIS EQUIPMENT

Redlegs

The U.S. Artillery from the Civil War to the Spanish–American War, 1861–1898

John P. Langellier

CHELSEA HOUSE PUBLISHERS
PHILADELPHIA

First Chelsea House hardback edition published 2000.

Library of Congress Cataloging-in-Publication Data
Langellier, J. Philip.
Redlegs: the U.S. artillery from the Civil War to the Spanish-American War, 1861–1898 / John P. Langellier.
   p.   cm.— (The G.I. series ; 11)
Originally published: London: Greenhill Books, © 1998.
Includes index.
Summary: A history of the artillery of the United States Army from 1861 to 1898 focusing on its uniforms and equipment.
ISBN 0-7910-5375-X
1. United States. Army—Artillery—History—19th century. 2. United States. Army—Uniforms—History—19th century. 3. United States. Army—Equipment—History—19th century. 4. United States—History—Civil War,1861–1865. 5. United States—History 1865–1898. [1. United States. Army—Artillery—History. 2. United States. Army—Uniforms—History. 3. United States. Army—Equipment—History.
4. United States—History—Civil War, 1861–1865.
5. United States—History—1865–1898.]
I. Title. II. Series.
UF23. L36 1999
358'. 1214'0973—dc21   99-14390
                       CIP

DEDICATION

This book is dedicated to Robert G. Borrell, Sr. for his years of preserving the history of the U.S. Artillery.

ACKNOWLEDGEMENTS AND ABBREVIATIONS

The author wishes to thank the following individuals and staffs of the institutions listed below:

AMWH	Autry Museum of Western Heritage, Los Angeles, CA
BU	Brown University Library, Anne S. K. Brown Collection
FAM	Frontier Army Museum, Fort Leavenworth, KS
FSHM	Fort Sam Houston Museum, San Antonio, TX
JG	Jerome Greene Collection
LC	Library of Congress
MJM	Dr. Michael J. McAfee Collection
NA	National Archives, Washington, D. C.
NPS	National Park Service, Golden Gate National Recreation Area
RBM	Reno Battlefield Museum, Garryowen, MT
RGB	Robert G. Borrell, Sr. Collection
SAHS	St. Augustine Historical Society
SDHS	San Diego Historical Society
UK	University of Kansas Libraries,Kansas Collection, Joseph Pennell Collection, Lawrence, KS
USAMHI	U.S. Army Military History Institute, Carlisle Barracks, PA
USAQM	U.S. Army Quartermaster Museum, Fort Lee, VA
USCM	U.S. Cavalry Museum, Fort Riley, KS
WCC	Western Costume Company, North Hollywood, CA

Designed and edited by DAG Publications Ltd
Designed by David Gibbons
Layout by Anthony A. Evans
Printed in Hong Kong

REDLEGS
THE U.S. ARTILLERY FROM THE CIVIL WAR TO THE SPANISH–AMERICAN WAR, 1861–1898

War clouds had been gathering in the U.S.A. for decades, when on 26 December 1860 Major Robert Anderson of the First U.S. Artillery informed his superiors in Washington D.C. that he had decided to withdraw the garrison of Fort Moultrie, South Carolina under the cover of darkness. Anderson and approximately seventy men relocated to nearby Fort Sumter, just a mile away in Charleston harbor. Civilian representatives from the Palmetto State (South Carolina) told federal officials they viewed this as a hostile act.

The major's superior, Virginia-born Secretary of War John B. Floyd, soon sent an angry telegram to his subordinate: 'Intelligence has reached here this morning that you have abandoned Fort Moultrie, spiked your guns, burned the carriages, and gone to Fort Sumter.... Explain the meaning of this report.'

Simply put, the long-simmering cauldron of sectional differences between the North and South was about to boil over. On 10 April 1861 Anderson received an ultimatum to vacate Sumter, which by that point had been surrounded by South Carolinian earthen emplacements. Two days later, at 4:30 a.m., an opening salvo from a 10-inch mortar struck the parade ground of Fort Sumter. The American Civil War had begun.

The five-sided Fort Sumter did not respond for three hours. Even then, only twenty-one of its cannon were in a position to answer the enemy, these being protected to a certain degree by their placement in the second tier of the fort's casemates. The twenty-seven guns atop the fort on the rampart *en barbette*, however, were too exposed to be safely manned. This fact, the small size of the Union garrison (just eighty-five officers, non-commissioned officers, and men), and a limited supply of ammunition, meant only a half-

dozen pieces fought back against the Confederate positions. In addition, expected reinforcements did not arrive.

The next day the situation worsened. Rebel artillerymen poured hot shot (heated rounds intended to set fire to buildings, ships, and the like) into the besieged fortress. These incendiaries ignited wooden structures which began to blaze fiercely. Finally, the defenders were forced to surrender. Anderson and his command evacuated the battered bastion at noon on 14 April, after some 4,000 enemy rounds had pummeled Sumter over a 34-hour period.

The intensity of the shelling demonstrated the firepower and hence the devastation that Yankee and Rebel gunners would wield over the next four years. In fact, soon after the outbreak of hostilities, the Regular Army expanded with the addition of the Fifth U.S. Artillery Regiment which joined the other four existing regiments.

Regardless of regiment, the backbone of the Union field artillery was the 12-pound smoothbore howitzer, commonly referred to as the 'Napoleon.' Of lesser importance, although a significant technological achievement of the time, was the 3-inch rifled ordnance gun. Both these pieces were muzzle-loaders, as were the other standard field artillery guns of the time: the 6- and 12-pounder guns; the mobile 12-pound mountain howitzer; the 12-, 24-, and 32-pound howitzers; and the 10- and 20-pound Parrott rifles. The Parrotts and ordnance rifles were iron or steel and rifled; the remaining weapons were all bronze smoothbores. Taken together, these ten basic types supposedly fired '90 per cent of the battlefield rounds' of the war.

If this figure rings true, the other 10 per cent would have been from several 'non-standard' guns, ranging from the 12- and 24-pound cast bronze James, to the 6- and 12-pound coast-steel Wiard. There also were 6- and 12-pound Whitworths, and a muzzle-loading 12-pound model of the same make. Two versions of 3-inch Armstrongs were also on hand, once again as muzzle-loader and breech-loader models. Other options were the 12-pound Wakley, the 3.67 Small Sawyer, and Coehorn mortars, the brass 24-pounder which weighed 296 pounds if mounted on an oak bed. There were even a few multiple-fire weapons, such as the Gatling gun, in the inventory, but these were really of little consequence.

The light, horse, and field artillerymen drew on a wide range of ordnance, yet their maximum effective range was about the same for most weapons, smoothbores reaching around 1,500 yards and rifles about 2,500 yards, all depending on the type of round fired. These included solid shot, canister, grape, shell, chain, and bar shot.

The heavy artillerymen, who defended forts or conducted sieges, manned 8- and 10-inch barbette-mounted seacoast howitzers, as well as 8-, 10-, and 12-inch Columbiads. There were also 32- and 42-pound seacoast guns; and a variety of Armstrong, Blakely, Dahlgren, Parrott, Rodman, and Whitworth models, too. Such pieces might send a 45- or 90-pound projectile some 2,000 yards. One of the huge Parrotts, an 8-incher weighing in at 16,300 pounds, was even given a name – 'The Swamp Angel' – because it was transported over marshlands by Union forces to hurl 175-pound shells into Charleston, South Carolina. In addition, 13-inch mortars were available. Among these was 'The Dictator' which at Petersburg, Virginia sent its projectiles for more than a mile to land in the besieged Rebel city. Although not mobile like the field guns, such payloads rained devastation in the hands of properly trained and experienced crews.

Indeed, many a Confederate fell to death-dealing Union 'redlegs' during the course of the war. After that bloody conflict ended, some military leaders began to consider the terrible lessons that were to be learned in the aftermath of the fighting. For one thing, the so-called 'third-system' brick forts such as Sumter had been rendered obsolete. Dispersed earthen berms with protected magazines and other innovations were seen as replacements for defensive works around key waterways and harbors. Breech-loading guns, including steel models, began to be considered as replacements for the old iron smoothbores. Innovative carriages were introduced, such as 'disappearing' models that allowed a piece to remain hidden from enemy view until heavy weights were released and the gun swung into position to fire, when it retracted once more out of sight from enemy warships. Further, improved propellants sent larger rounds further then ever, sometimes up to several miles. Even a pneumatic-air 'dynamite' gun that fired charges of that lethal new explosive was considered. So, too, was reinforced concrete, which was introduced to build coastal batteries towards the end of the 19th century. Many of these advancements took place during the administration of Secretary of War William Endicott, thereby giving rise to references to the 'Endicott' era of coastal defenses. With Endicott, U.S. coastal defense had entered a new period.

Although the heavy artillery underwent tremendous transformation, field artillery innovation did not move as rapidly. Although 1-inch, as well as .45 and .50 caliber Gatling guns were issued, the 12-pound mountain howitzer, along with the 12-pound 'Napoleon' and an occasional small mortar, remained standard for several decades after the Civil War. This rather static situation for the field artillery partially stemmed from the lack of a conventional enemy against which such weapons could be deployed in the decades following Robert E. Lee's surrender. From the late 1860s until the early 1890s, a major mission of the army was the pursuit of various American Indian groups across the Trans-Mississippi West.

Only on rare occasions did an elusive adversary stand and fight. A notable exception to this occurred in the wake of an event that began in September 1872. At that time a U.S. Army officer, Major John Green, attempted to speak to one of the leaders of the Modocs, an Indian people who made their home in northern California and southern Oregon. Major Green wanted their leaders to discuss accusations made against the Modocs, but efforts to parlay with one of their headmen, known as Captain Jack, proved fruitless.

Within weeks Green's superior, Brigadier General E.R.S. Canby, decided to press the issue. He sent orders for the arrest of Captain Jack and two others, Black Jim and Scarface Charley. After entering the Modoc camp, an exchange of fire took place, leaving casualties on both sides. The Modocs fled. A war had begun.

In the confusion, Jack escaped, as did many

others of the band. The Modocs eventually regrouped in the region south of Tule Lake, which some had called 'hell with the fire burnt out.' Here in the black lava that nature had formed into natural fortifications, the Modocs made their stand.

Weeks passed before the U.S. government's forces arrived on the scene, allowing the Modocs to prepare for the siege which ensued. Regulars and volunteers eventually surrounded them. After their first attack on 17 January 1873, the troops found the Modocs to be tenacious fighters. The opening engagement ended in a clear victory for the lava bed's defenders, despite the fact that they were outnumbered by an estimated seven to one.

The Modocs continued to hold their own against cavalry, infantry, and militiamen from Oregon and California. Mortars and mountain howitzers, along with crews from the Fourth U.S. Artillery stationed at the Presidio of San Francisco, joined the attack, but their guns did not dislodge the inflexible Modocs.

Determined to remain free, the Modocs successfully fought from their entrenched positions.

For most of the conflict, public opinion was in the Modocs' favor. Then, on Good Friday, 11 April 1873, Canby and a small party of commissioners went to speak with Captain Jack. In the midst of the talks Captain Jack pulled out a concealed weapon and fired point blank into Canby's face, signaling a general attack on the U.S. representatives. When the slaughter stopped, Canby and two of his fellow negotiators were dead.

Sympathy towards the Modocs ceased as Canby's successor redoubled efforts to dislodge the enemy. After considerable bloodshed, fighting, and the roar of artillery, the ill-fated Modoc survivors capitulated on 1 June 1873. A trial followed, and Captain Jack and three others were sentenced to execution. The remaining 153 Modocs suffered a different fate: relocation to the Quapaw Indian Agency in today's Oklahoma. After that there were few other noteworthy instances of artillery's use against native peoples.

A brief experiment starting in 1878, presaged future developments, however, when a platoon made up of black enlisted men from the Twenty-fourth U.S. Infantry were formed on an experimental basis to man Gatling guns. These foot soldiers were attached to Battery F, Second Artillery, where they responded well to training. The unit impressed some high ranking officers

who succeeded in having the organization posted in 1881 to the newly-established Cavalry and Infantry School at Fort Leavenworth, Kansas. A half-dozen years later the Cavalry and Light Artillery School was founded at Fort Riley, Kansas.

These schools and the Gatling battery were clear efforts to improve the state of the field artillery, and ready it for a battle against a conventional foe. In the meantime, U.S. artillerymen were to play a role in the tragic clash that took place in the winter of 1890 at Wounded Knee, South Dakota. There a weary, cold band of Minneconjou Lakotas encamped after being brought to bay by troopers of the Seventh U.S. Cavalry. Besides the men from George Custer's old regiment, Battery E, First U.S. Artillery kept watch over the village.

Tensions ran high. Both sides were on edge. On 29 December the soldiers attempted to disarm the men of the village. A rifle shot triggered a brief, costly fight. Battery E opened up its 1.65-inch rapid-fire breech-loading Hotchkiss guns, bringing deadly fire to bear. When the firing stopped, half of the village lay dead on the frozen ground, an estimated 153 in all, and many were wounded, some lingering before they too perished. Twenty-five soldiers were killed in the exchange and another thirty-nine were wounded. The 'wagon-guns' had contributed to the death not only of a people, but also a dream. The Ghost Dance that had set in motion the course of events which ended at Wounded Knee was to be the last great resistance of the Sioux nation.

The Hotchkiss guns at Wounded Knee weighed 241 pounds and could launch their 2-pound fused projectile up to 3,500 yards. This relatively light piece, along with 3.2-inch 'bag guns', were among the field artillery breech-loaders that were introduced in the 1880s as the American military attempted to keep pace with technology. The 'bag gun' was an improvement over previous arms in that it was a breech-loader. Neither weapon had a recoil system, however. Additionally, the puff of black powder gave away the gun's position to the enemy.

This was particularly a drawback when facing a foe that had smokeless powder guns. In 1898 that was just the situation when war with Spain caused the United States to send troops to Cuba, Puerto Rico, and the Philippines. On 8 March 1898, as a prelude to conflict, Congress authorized two new regiments of artillery, the Sixth and the Seventh. These units and the five existing regiments, had to contend with Spanish gunners who had a number of smokeless powder pieces, although their ordnance inventory ran the gamut from antiquated 18th-century bronze cannon, to up-to-date breech-loaders made by Krupp. In all, four field artillery batteries, a Gatling gun battery, and two siege artillery batteries went to Cuba.

As one example of the light artillery's role in the Cuban campaign, they were called upon to support an assault against some 500 Spanish troops who held a strong defensive point with barbed wire protection at El Caney. At first, the American artillery were badly deployed, so they proved ineffective. Later, with the guns relocated to a more forward position, the shelling was highly successful, and helped bring about the fall of Santiago's outer defenses.

Previously, the Gatling gun detachment, under Lieutenant John Parker, had realized the importance of close support in the assault at San Juan. The firepower of these weapons aided the offensive momentum that eventually carried the day.

In the end American military might prevailed, and Madrid capitulated. The United States had won its 'splendid little war.'

The peace after this victory proved short-lived in that the people of Spain's former possessions, the Philippines, balked at replacing one foreign master with another. Intent on independence, on 4 February 1899 Filipinos began a determined struggle to drive the newcomers away. Fighting both offensive and defensive battles, the Filipino military kept the United States Army occupied in many parts of the islands. In one instance the Sultan of Bayan commanded a formidable Moro army who held out in their *cottas*, or forts, armed with small cannon known locally as *lentakas*. Captain William Sharp McNair's mountain battery had a hot time when, along with elements of the Tenth and Seventeenth Infantry and Fifteenth Cavalry, they attempted to dislodge the Moros.

Captain McNair's colleague, Captain Victor H. Bridgeman, found the Philippines a challenge as well. His Light Battery G, Sixth U.S. Artillery, came into the country with a half-dozen 3.2-inchers. Eventually, four Hotchkiss 1.65-inch guns were added. The larger guns required draft animals which were in short supply at first. Small local ponies were pressed into service, but when they were found wanting, Brahma bulls had to be used as replacements until mules could be obtained.

Finding stock was only part of the challenge. The eight guns were divided and sent with two columns on operations that took the artillerymen over 400 miles. Along the way these gunners participated in some thirty engagements against the Filipinos.

By this time the United States was a major military power. In keeping with its new stature, coastal artillery advances continued including increased use of electricity, torpedoes, and mines. New, improved weapons were also obtained.

Additionally, the Artillery School at Fort Monroe, Virginia, formed part of a developing army-wide system of military education. Institutions such as the School of Submarine Defense at Fort Totten, New York, and the School of Application for Cavalry and Field Artillery at Fort Riley were established. The Field Artillery School that evolved from a practical course of conduct of fire was set up at Fort Sill, Oklahoma, early in the 20th century. As the new century dawned, the American artillerymen was well established, but some of his greatest challenges were yet to come.

For Further Reading

Boatner, Mark M. III. *The Civil War Dictionary.* New York: David Mckay Company, Inc., 1959.

Downey, Fairfax. *Cannonade: Great Artillery Actions of History.* Garden City, NY: Doubleday and Company, 1966.

Lewis, Emanuel R. *Seacoast Defences of the United States: An Introductory History.* Washington, D.C: Smithsonian Institution Press, 1970.

Stevens, Phillip H. *Artillery Through the Ages.* New York: Franklin Watts, Inc., 1965.

A light artillery sergeant in the 1861 through 1872 dress uniform, holding the M1840 light artillery saber. (RGB)

Left: An enlisted man's light artillery dress cap manufactured during the Civil War, with worsted scarlet cords and horsetail plume. (RGB)

Left: Russian knot variations as worn by light artillery officers from 1860 through 1872. (RGB)

Right: Epaulets of a second lieutenant of the First U.S. Artillery, and shoulder straps of a second lieutenant of artillery in a black japanned tin carrying-case of the Civil War era. (RGB)

Right: According to General Order No. 6, War Department, 13 March 1861, the 1858-pattern enlisted heavy artillery hat was to loop on the left side, and be held in place by a stamped sheet brass 'eagle' measuring 2½-inches high by 2-inches wide. Further, the hat was to have scarlet worsted cords ending in tassels. The battery letter (1-inch high) and regimental number (⅝-inches long) were to appear with the crossed cannon insignia (3½-inch long from muzzle to breech crossed at the trunnions) of artillery on the front of the hat, although the regimental numeral is lacking here. (RGB)

Left: A heavy artillery sergeant in the dress uniform of the 1861 through 1872 era, with the M1833 non-commissioned officers' short sword unique to that branch. (USAQM)

Above: Left to right: sergeant of light artillery, private of light artillery, corporal of heavy artillery, and musician or trumpeter of heavy artillery, all in the 1881 through 1884 dress uniform. (LC)

Right: In the late 1870s the practice of lining capes of overcoats in flannel to correspond with branch colors was approved. This sergeant of heavy artillery wears a scarlet-lined cape with his 1881-pattern spiked dress helmet. Chevrons were to be worn on the overcoat points down above the elbow until 1883, when the position was lowered to between the elbow and the cuff (although the 19th-century artist who rendered this illustration did not depict the chevrons). The combination of dress helmet and great coat was not common. (BU)

Above: An illustration by H.A. Ogden of the 1885 through 1903 dress uniform. A private of heavy artillery (left foreground) approaches a group of non-commissioned officers. The center NCO is a sergeant-major of heavy artillery as indicated by his three stripes of gold lace surmounted by an arc of three stripes on a scarlet background. He also has one service stripe displayed on his lower sleeve to indicate the completion of one enlistment (either a three- or five-year period). Next to him, a first sergeant of light artillery, with three stripes and a lozenge above on his sleeve, cradles an M1840 light artillery saber. The figure on the far right is a sergeant of ordnance. Light and heavy artillery troops appear in the background, including a musician with scarlet herringbone trim on his chest. (WCC)

Top right: In 1898 most artillery dress uniforms were packed away in exchange for combat uniforms, including the new khaki trimmed with scarlet for artillery depicted in a lithograph of the Spanish-American War era. (WCC)

Right: Manning 3.2-inch 'bag guns,' artillerymen wear the khaki breeches that became available from 1898, and the 1883-pattern blue wool field shirt, a combination that saw considerable use during the Spanish-American War and the years which immediately followed. (RGB)

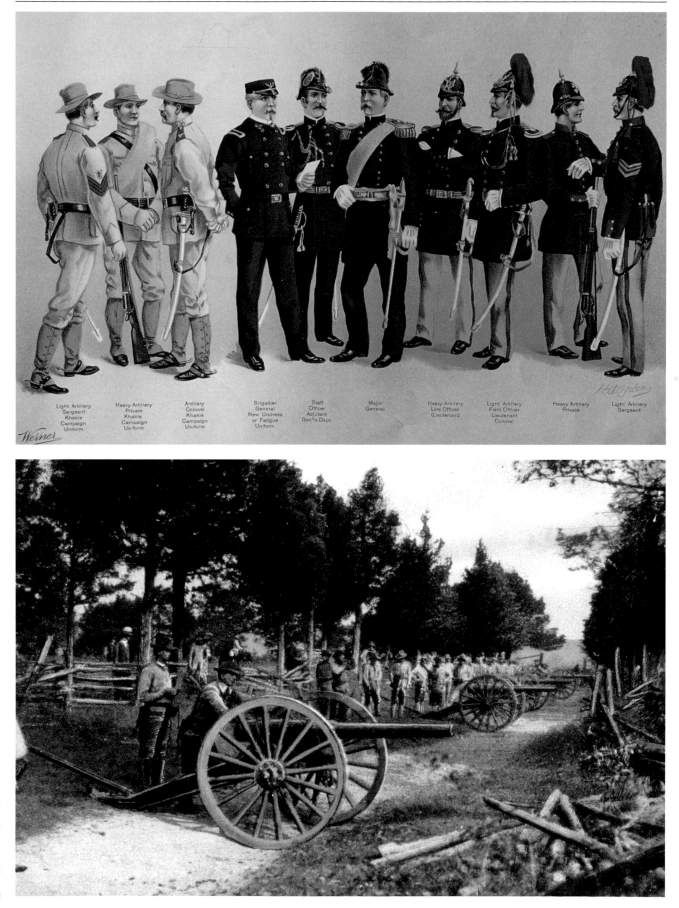

Werner

Light Artillery
Sergeant
Khakie
Campaign
Uniform

Heavy Artillery
Private
Khakie
Campaign
Uniform

Artillery
Colonel
Khakie
Campaign
Uniform

Brigadier
General
New Undress
or Fatigue
Uniform

Staff
Officer
Adjutant
Gen'ls Dept.

Major
General

Heavy Artillery
Line Officer
(Lieutenant)

Light Artillery
Field Officer
Lieutenant
Colonel

Heavy Artillery
Private

Light Artillery
Sergeant

Right: The sky-blue wool trousers or breeches with 1½-inch scarlet stripes of facing material, and the dark blue wool 1895-pattern officers' jacket with black mohair trim and shoulder straps with scarlet centers, were also retained for combat. They are worn here with the 1889 or 1899-pattern campaign hat. (WCC)

Left: Electrician sergeants were authorized for heavy artillery in 1899. Insignia on the dress uniform consisted of white silk embroidered lightning bolts, to be worn over the 1884-pattern bullion sergeants' chevrons on a scarlet facing material background. (RGB)

Above: From 1858 through 1861 the color of 'trowsers' (as they were usually referred to in 19th-century regulations) for heavy artillery enlisted men and officers was to be dark blue. That color was changed to sky-blue by General Orders No. 108, Headquarters of the Army, 16 December 1861. In addition, officers were to have an ⅛-inch welt of scarlet let into the outer seams. These officers of the Third U.S. Artillery wear both hues of blue in their dress uniform. All wear the 1858-pattern hat looped up on the right side as prescribed by regulations, although some of the men have creased their crowns, which was not regulation. The man second from the left wears his crimson silk sash 'scarf' fashion to designate his service as 'officer of the day.' With one exception, they are all captains, and wear the single-breasted company grade (second lieutenant through captain) frock coat. The central figure is Major Henry S. Burton, a field grade officer (majors through colonels) who, in keeping with his rank, wears a double-breasted frock coat with seven buttons in each row. (SDHS, Ticor Collection)

Right: A cape could be worn with the 1851-pattern officers' overcoat, 'of the same color and material as the coat, removable at the pleasure of the wearer, and reaching to the cuff of the coat-sleeve when the arm is extended.' (RGB)

Right: A long black silk 'loop *à l'échelle* without tassel or plate' was to be placed at the throat of the cloak coat and the optional detachable matching cape for officers. (RGB)

Left: This field grade officer wears the dark blue trousers of the 1858–61 period, and the double-breasted 1851-pattern frock coat with the crimson silk sash wrapped twice about the waist and tied slightly behind the left hip. Gold epaulets served for full dress occasions. The sword is the M1850 staff and field. The 1858-pattern hat is creased in the middle and upturned on both sides, in many respects resembling a version of this headpiece referred to as the 'Burnside' pattern, after Union Major General Ambrose Burnside. Although the gauntlets were not regulation, they were a relatively common addition to officers' uniforms during the Civil War. (RGB)

Below: This Union field grade officer from the Third Rhode Island Heavy Artillery, has dispensed with the 1858-pattern hat and epaulets, and has shoulder straps and the forage cap with sloping visor that came to be called the 'McDowell' cap, after Union Major General Irvin McDowell. Once more, gauntlets are evident. (RGB)

Above: This field grade officer has the double-breasted frock coat prescribed for his rank and shoulder straps with scarlet center and double gold-embroidered borders, these additional borders being more costly than the single border type that were commonly worn. The leaves were gold for majors and silver for lieutenant colonels, one leaf being positioned at each end of the strap. A large silver-embroidered spread eagle worked into the center of the scarlet backing was the insignia of a colonel. (RGB)

Left: For inclement weather an oilcloth cover could be placed over the forage cap, this style being one with a 'McDowell' pattern worn by this field grade artillery officer. (MJM)

Right: Major Solomon Giles, Second New York Light Artillery Regiment, has selected a dark slouch hat rather than the regulation 1858-pattern hat or forage cap as his field headgear, a practice that many others followed during the Civil War. He cradles an M1859 light cavalry saber with gold officers' saber knot. The major also has a holster for his cap-and-ball revolver strapped at the right hip, although his pistol is butt backward rather than the traditional butt forward style worn by military men of the Civil War era. (RGB)

Left: A portrait of Major John Fulton Reynolds, commandant of cadets at the U.S. Military Academy in 1860. Note the silver embroidered '3' in the center (for Third U.S. Artillery Regiment) of the artillery insignia on the 1858-pattern hat. There are no rank insignia on the gold epaulets, these being blank for second lieutenants and majors, save for a circle of scarlet with a gold embroidered regimental numeral and a border around the scarlet of silver embroidery. The size of the bullion fringe on the epaulets distinguished subalterns from majors, the former having an ⅛-inch diameter fringe and the latter a ½-inch diameter fringe. (USAMHI)

Above: Lieutenant Henry C. Symonds, Second U.S. Artillery, has looped up his 1858-pattern hat on the left side contrary to regulations. The pair of black ostrich feathers are visible on the right, although these were to be placed on the left side according to General Orders No. 4, Headquarters of the Army, 26 February 1861. Symonds also wears an old pattern interlocking belt plate of the type worn from the 1820s through the Mexican War, rather than the 1851-pattern rectangular plate with spread eagle and wreath depicted in the other images of officers in this volume. His saber is the M1859-pattern cavalry weapon, and his trousers are the old dark blue style worn early in the Civil War. (MJM)

Above: A civilian-style slouch hat serves as the campaign hat for this first lieutenant of artillery who has added his shoulder straps over the top of the epaulets for this portrait, although he probably would not have worn the combination in tandem on duty. Straps were designed to replace epaulets for field and most garrison wear, and both items were designed to be removable. Note also the ⅛-inch scarlet welt on the trousers called for in regulations to designate artillery officers. (RGB)

Above: Company grade officers like Second Lieutenant Howard Mather Burnham, Battery H, Fifth U.S. Artillery, regularly wore the 1851-pattern single-breasted frock coat with nine artillery officers' gilt buttons. Burnham, who was killed at Chickamauga, Georgia on 19 September 1863, wears blank shoulder straps with scarlet centers as rank indicators. He has purchased short riding gloves and an M1840 light artillery saber. It appears that there are two ventilators in the top of his forage cap to allow better circulation. This idea was later incorporated into some regulation headgear from the 1870s. (RGB)

Top right: This second lieutenant of the Second U.S. Artillery has a more typical forage cap, but has obtained an M1859 light cavalry saber and gauntlets with large cuffs. (RGB)

Right: First Lieutenant Henry C. Babcock, Twelfth New York Light Artillery opted for a low-crowned French-inspired chasseur forage cap. He has evidently turned down the standing collar of his frock coat, thereby exposing the velvet lining, or it is possible that this is a dark velvet-covered roll collar, a feature that some officers preferred. The cap device is somewhat unusual in that oval backgrounds tended to be the norm, not rectangular ones. (RGB)

Above: This artillery second lieutenant's saber belt is stitched with white thread and has a shoulder straps attached at the left hip and the rear similar to the later 'Sam Browne' belt in order to help keep the saber from pulling downward. The slouch hat has gold and black officers' hat cords, and crossed gold embroidered artillery cannon insignia, although the silver regimental numeral is not displayed. (RGB)

Above right: This first lieutenant of artillery also had a cross strap with his sword belt. His silver regimental numeral appears above the crossed canon insignia on his forage cap. The two stripes on his lower sleeves are unusual, in that service chevrons of this type were worn by enlisted men, but were not prescribed for officers of the Regular Army. During the Civil War, however, numerous variations existed. (RGB)

Right: Prior to the Civil War light artillery officers were given permission to don a short 'stable' jacket much like the 1854-pattern enlisted jacket, but without the scarlet worsted lace. The stable jacket had nine buttons like the frock coat, rather than twelve buttons as was the case with the enlisted mounted artillery jacket. This unidentified Union horse artillery officer has also procured gauntlets, tall riding boots, and an M1859 cavalry saber. (RGB)

Above right: First Lieutenant David Hammel, Sixth New York Heavy Artillery, wears the jacket rather than the frock coat more commonly worn by siege or heavy artillery subalterns. Additionally, he had gold braid galloons added to his sleeves to indicate his rank, although his shoulder straps with their scarlet backing and single gold bar at each end already indicate his status. While boots and short jackets were actually the norm for light artillery battery officers during the Civil War, these items also proved popular with officers of heavy or siege artillery batteries. (USAMHI)

Right: Officers serving with Regular Army horse artillery batteries were authorized a cap with falling scarlet horsehair and gold cords with sidelines as worn by these company grade officers. The man on the left has the M1859 cavalry saber, and the man on the right the M1840 light artillery saber. (MJM)

Right: The light artillery officers' cap, worn here by a second lieutenant of the Fifth U.S. Artillery. Some officers' caps, as seen here, had leather tops similar to the enlisted models, while others had tops to the crown that were of the same material as the body of the cap. Officers' cords were gold. (RGB)

Left: Shoulder straps with scarlet centers were the typical means of indicating artillery officers' rank in the field, but from 1860 through 1872, light artillery officers were permitted to wear Russian knots made of gold cord to depict their rank. Captain Hiram E. Sickles, Seventeenth Independent Battery, New York Light Artillery (Orleans Battery) wears this alternative insignia. (RGB)

Left: A slightly different form of the Russian knot is worn by an officer, probably from the Ninth Massachusetts Battery, who also had flat gold lace added to his forage cap. (RGB)

Right: Russian knots top the shoulders of this artillery officer, whose crossed cannon insignia are centered in a gold embroidered wreath, an arrangement more typically associated with staff officers. His jacket had black or dark blue velvet cuffs, and a breast pocket closed with the artillery officers' small gilt button. (RGB)

Above: In some instances Russian knots were even employed on the four-button sack coat. This artillery officer's sack coat has long skirts and two slash pockets, practical additions not found in the regulation pattern of the era. (RGB)

Above: A second lieutenant of artillery nonchalantly poses with his four-button sack coat open except at the top, to reveal his vest (waistcoat). Vests were optional wear, usually in blue or buff, and were of civilian cut, but usually had military buttons. Once again, the skirts of the sack coat tended to be longer than the typical style of the Civil War. (RGB)

Right: The silver embroidered '3' on the low-crown chasseur forage cap indicates this second lieutenant's regiment. A white short cravat, and civilian-type sack coat with lapels that appear to be edged or bound, demonstrates the rather casual mix of military and non-military clothing items that were worn by Civil War artillery officers and others. (RGB)

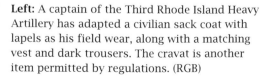

Left: A captain of the Third Rhode Island Heavy Artillery has adapted a civilian sack coat with lapels as his field wear, along with a matching vest and dark trousers. The cravat is another item permitted by regulations. (RGB)

Above: By the mid-Civil War officers could dispense with shoulder straps if they wished in order to present less of a target to the enemy. Here, a Union artillery captain wears only the double bars of his rank, which were less conspicuous than straps; later in the century, straps were abolished on field wear in favor of rank insignia. The white trousers, usually of cotton, but sometimes of linen, had been authorized for the Artillery School garrison in the 1850s, and remained a practical, albeit non-regulation clothing item for Civil War troops serving in hot climates. (RGB)

Above: Additional scarlet worsted lace was applied to the front of 1854-pattern light artillery jackets for musicians and buglers. Trousers were plain sky-blue, but sometimes stripes were worn by bandsmen and musicians, as is the case here where the stripes may be scarlet on each side with a white center. (RGB)

Right: When a regulation 1858-pattern hat was not available, or because of individual tastes, fur-felt civilian slouch hats could be trimmed with scarlet worsted cords terminating in tassels, sheet brass insignia, and black ostrich feathers to provide a suitably military piece of headgear. Also note that this man has looped his hat on the right as yet another deviation from regulations. (RGB)

Above: A heavy artillery musician wears the 1858-pattern frock coat with extra scarlet trim on the chest, as well as the scarlet facing material piping around the collar and on each cuff. Once more, the multi-color leg stripes are not according to regulation, but were not uncommon given the wide latitude of uniform options granted to bandsmen during the Civil War. The forage cap was one of a number of types of headgear worn with the frock coat. (RGB)

Above: Another type of headgear worn with the 1858-pattern frock coat was the 1858-pattern hat for heavy artillery, such as this one photographed in this *carte de visite* of a corporal of the Eighth New York Heavy Artillery Regiment, Company M. A single ostrich feather was to be worn on the left side by enlisted men and the hat pinned up on the right, contrary to regulations calling for just the opposite configuration. The brass shoulder scales are of the pattern for musicians, privates, and corporals. (RGB)

Right: This private of the heavy artillery wears a 'Burnside' type hat instead of the 1858-pattern regulation hat, or else has creased the crown of his regulation hat. He does abide by regulations in all other respects, however, including looping the hat on the left side and attaching the black ostrich feather to the right. (MJM)

Right: U.S. Army regulations only called for a company letter to be worn on the enlisted 1858-pattern forage cap, but in this case an artillery-man has added crossed cannon to the front of his chasseur-style cap. He also holds an M1840 musician's sword, which may be a photographer's prop because there are no other indications that this individual was a musician. (RGB)

Left: This heavy artillery private has added both the regimental number and crossed cannon insignia to the crown of his standard 'bummer's' (forage) cap – a fairly common deviation from regulations. (RGB)

Right: A private of the heavy or siege artillery displays the scarlet service stripes below the elbow to indicate completion of five years' faithful service. He wears a dark blue vest, another option that many enlisted men purchased to add to their kit. An impressive watch chain is attached to the vest. (RGB)

Left: A sergeant, possibly of the Fourth U.S. Artillery, Company A, in the 1858-pattern frock coat, with the scarlet worsted chevrons worn points down above the elbows on each arm to indicate his rank. (RGB)

Right: Regimental non-commissioned offices were to have silk chevrons: this regimental quartermaster sergeant has three stripes pointing down and three tie bars above on his custom four-button sack coat with breast pocket. The small cannon on his hat are also specially made, not being of the type issued to most rank-and-file. The 1½-inch worsted scarlet trousers stripes prescribed for all sergeants of artillery are visible, too. (RGB)

Left: This corporal of light artillery appears to be wearing a sky-blue vest over what seems to be a dark blue flannel shirt with piping, both dapper non-regulation clothing items. The scarlet worsted chevrons, however, are correct for a corporal. The two service stripes below the elbows should have indicated the completion of ten years' services, although given the youthful appearance of this individual it is more likely that they symbolize a lesser time of active duty. The crossed cannon insignia on the chasseur forage cap are also not typical, being more like officers' styles. Finally, the scarlet worsted trousers stripe seems to be wider than the ½-inch called for in U.S. Army regulations for corporals. The insignia on the right breast is a commercially purchased identification badge – rather like a precursor to 'dogtags.' (RGB)

Right: The waist of this light artillery private's jacket from Battery H of an unknown regiment is slightly curved. Usually 1854-pattern light artillery jackets were cut at an angle, but numerous manufacturers made uniforms during the Civil War and this resulted in a number of variations. Note also that the trousers have additional sky-blue cloth reinforcement inside to prolong use during mounted service. (MJM)

Above left: This private of Battery I of an an unknown regiment holds the M1840 light artillery saber. (Russ Yeagy Collection, USMHI)

Above right: In addition to the 1854-pattern jacket, light artillerymen could wear the scarlet horsehair plume-topped cap with scarlet worsted cords as demonstrated by this sergeant of the Second U.S. Artillery *c.* 1865. (USMHI)

Opposite page, left: The stamped brass eagle insignia, the regimental numeral, and crossed cannon can clearly be seen on this enlisted light artillery cap, as can the 'tulip' which held the horsetail plume. (MJM)

Opposite page, right: An unidentified bandmaster or chief musician has donned the light artillery cap as his smart headgear, but wears the 1858-pattern heavy artillery enlisted frock coat, with scarlet piping on the cuffs and around the collar. (MJM)

Above: This light artillery private wears service stripes on his 1854-pattern jacket, presumably of scarlet to indicate the completion of service in an artillery organization. He substitutes a civilian hat for military issue headgear, but has added issue insignia. His belt is an officers' type, and is perhaps a prop borrowed from the photographer. (RGB)

Left: One more deviation from regulation is seen in the case of this corporal who has tucked his four-button sack coat into his dark blue trousers, or has had it modified into a shirt by cutting down the skirt. The hat is a non-issue civilian slouch hat fitted with stamped brass crossed cannon. He carries the M1840 light artillery saber. (RGB)

Right: Another artillery private wears a variant of the light artillery jacket without worsted scarlet trim. In addition, he appears to have two service stripes on each cuff, although they are not angled according to regulations (higher point at the front rather than the rear). The cap insignia is gold embroidery typical of devices worn by officers, but unusual for enlisted men. (RGB)

Below: Manning a 3-inch Parrott Rifle, this artillery crew exhibits both regulation four-button sack coats and the 1854-pattern light artillery enlisted jacket. Some of the men have procured civilian slouch hats, while many others wear the standard issue forage cap. The Parrott was a wrought iron piece that could fire its projectile an average of 1,800 yards when elevated five degrees. (RGB)

Above: This 6-pound Wiard Rifle has a globe sight on the muzzle. A secondary field piece for the Union, the Wiard had a rifled steel barrel which when elevated five degrees had an average range of 1,800 yards. (RGB)

Opposite page, top: At Fredericksburg, Virginia Union heavy artillery gunners serve an iron 32-pounder on a siege carriage. An 8-pound charge propelled the projectile an average of 1,922 yards towards the enemy when elevated five degrees. Most of these heavy artillerymen have the four-button sack coat, while the officers wear the 1851-pattern company grade frock coat. (LC)

Right: The men of the First Connecticut Heavy Artillery stand ready to their 24-pounder siege guns at Fort Richardson, Virginia in the 1858-pattern frock coat paired with the bummer's caps. All have standard infantry accoutrements; it was not unusual to use heavy artillery troops as infantry when they were not serving their guns. In this instance, their pieces, such as the gun in the foreground, are mounted variously on siege carriages, or on barbette carriages, such as the one in the center position on the right wall. These iron 24-pounders had an average range of 1,901 yards when elevated five degrees. (LC)

Opposite page, top: Battery B, Second U.S. Artillery was a 'flying battery' in that all the men were mounted. They were ready to take their 3-inch wrought iron ordnance rifles into action at Fair Oaks, Virginia during June 1862. The guns fired a 6-pound projectile 1,800 yards when elevated five degrees. (LC)

Opposite page, bottom: A bronze 12-pound mountain howitzer, with caisson in the background and battery guidon in the foreground, is ready for action against Confederates. (RGB)

Above: Heavy artillery troops, probably at guard mount because the officer wears his crimson silk sash scarf fashion to indicate he is officer of the day, at Alcatraz Island in San Francisco Bay just after the Civil War. The M1833 short sword remained the edged weapon for heavy artillery sergeants of the time, and the 1858-pattern frock coat and hat were retained as well, until phased out after 1872. (NPS)

Right: Officers' 1851-pattern single-breasted frock coats were regulation for second lieutenants through captains until 1872. Here, it is worn by Second Lieutenant E.K. Russell, First U.S. Artillery. (RGB)

Left: While serving on Reconstruction duty in Louisiana, First Lieutenant Charles King (later transferred to the Fifth U.S. Cavalry and destined to become a noted novelist) wears the 1851-pattern frock coat and the low chasseur forage cap that grew in popularity during the Civil War and thereafter. He holds an M1859 cavalry officers' saber, one that appears to be a high grade type with extra ornamentation. The gold lace saber knot with bullion tassel prescribed for officers is also visible. (AMWH)

Right: Light artillery officers and enlisted men were to have this distinctive cap until 1872. This second lieutenant has also added foragers to his uniform, a practice that began in the Civil War and was carried on in the ensuing years, albeit without official approval. The saber is the new model adopted in 1872 for light artillery officers. (RBM)

Above: During the Modoc War of 1872–73, Fourth Artillery gunners were dispatched from the San Francisco Bay Area. Here, an artillery sergeant, (as indicated by his 1½-inch scarlet worsted trousers stripe and three chevrons on his four-button blouse) stands at the ready next to a 12-pound mountain howitzer, which could launch its projectile 900 yards at a five degree elevation. It was a primary weapon for the military in the West after the Civil War because of its mobility. The piece could be dismantled and carried on mules, or pulled if needed by conventional field artillery. This war was one of the few instances where artillery was used against American Indians in the post-Civil War era. (NA)

Left: Enlisted heavy artillerymen had their own longer-skirted coat with scarlet facings, and a stiff cap with scarlet braid topped by a scarlet pompon, according to the new 1872 regulations. This is a private of the Third U.S. Artillery with the new dress uniform. Note that he has two service stripes on his sleeves, indicating he is a veteran of ten years. (RGB)

Above: A company of heavy artillery were detailed to the U.S. Barracks St. Augustine, Florida after the Civil War, in this case falling out in the 1872-pattern dress uniform at 'parade rest.' Two officers stand with their backs to the camera as they review the troops, while two more officers stand directly in front of the troops they command. At the right are three non-commissioned officers holding M1840 NCO swords rather than the Springfield rifles carried by the privates and corporals. A number of the men wear the old over-the-shoulder cartridge box with cross belt and circular brass plate, indicating that this photograph was taken not long after the issue of the new uniform. (SAHS)

Below: This heavy artillery company had their image captured in the mid-1870s, the date being indicated by the presence of the Hagner cartridge boxes and brace system, and the rectangular belt plates and belts worn by the men. The company's first sergeant has four service stripes on his coat and holds the M1840 NCO sword, while the two buglers (in the next row center and closest to the wall) have M1840 musicians' swords. The buglers' coats were also to have scarlet 'herringbone' on the chest to distinguish them from the other ranks. (Old Fort Niagara Association)

Above: As had been the custom from early times, bandsmen continued to have considerable latitude in their uniform as long as it was sanctioned by the regimental commanding officer. In the case of the Third U.S. Artillery's band, their 1872-pattern dress uniform coat had scarlet trefoils rather than the standard company buglers' herringbone trim. (RGB)

Right: Second Lieutenant Daniel Morgan Taylor of the First Artillery wears the dress uniform typical of the heavy artillery company grade officers during the 1872 through 1880 period. Trouser stripes were to be of 1½-inch scarlet facing material. The cock feathers on his cap were to be scarlet. Field grade officers differed little from this look, except that their belts were of solid lace, and their coats featured three gold lace ornaments on each sleeve, rather than the two for lieutenants and captains, as seen on Taylor's coat. The field grade coat also had nine buttons in each row. (RBM)

Above: Company grade officers' coats of the 1872-pattern were double-breasted with seven artillery officers' buttons in each row. The coats of field grade officers, such as the individual standing third from the left next to the staff officer in his fore and aft *chapeau de bras*, had nine buttons in each row. (SAHS)

Right: Officers serving with light artillery batteries received a dress helmet in 1872 with scarlet horsetail plume and gold cords. The helmet plate bore the regimental number in silver, those for enlisted men being plain. The remainder of the dress uniform was essentially the same as for heavy artillery officers. For instance, the belt had three scarlet horizontal stripes intermixed with four of gold for company grade officers, as worn by this captain of the First U.S. Artillery. (NA)

Left: The 1874-pattern blouse had only five buttons and was of a streamlined cut without pleats. A pair of 1880 'Laidley' system ¾-inch square marksmanship buttons of sterling silver with the facsimile of a target on the face, is attached to each side of the collar. In turn, the collar is trimmed with scarlet cord, as were the cuffs of the blouse. The hat is the 1876-pattern campaign hat with 'Brasher' spinners (miniature fans) on each side of the crown theoretically to promote circulation. The 1876-pattern trousers are also seen here, one feature being flared cuffs. (RBM)

Above: While the coat remained little changed from 1872 to 1884 for enlisted heavy artillerymen, this private from the First U.S. Artillery holds one major element in the evolution of the dress uniform: the 1881 pattern helmet with spike and eagle plate. (RBM)

Left: In 1880 officers were to remove the gold lace from their dress coats. The following year the cap was replaced by a spiked helmet for heavy artillery officers. This remained the dress for the heavy artillery until 1902, although a slightly different arrangement was introduced in 1901, when regimental numerals in silver embroidery were discontinued on the scarlet-backed officers' shoulder knots. The material on the left arm and M1860 staff and field sword is black crepe, a sign of mourning that was permitted with officers' uniforms. (RGB)

Right: Captain Henry C. Cushing, Fourth U.S. Artillery Regiment, wearing the 1881 through 1902 mounted artillery officers' dress uniform. The boots are the M1889 pattern, and the gauntlets are possibly the 1886-pattern. (USAMHI)

Left: A light artillery crew stand next to their 3-inch ordnance rifle in their 1881-pattern dress helmets and 1885-pattern dress coats. By this period, issue gauntlets had replaced white 'Berlin' gloves. (FSHM)

Opposite page, bottom: Sergeant Benjamin Bowen wears the 1885-pattern light artillery dress uniform coat with full covered scarlet facings on the collar (the 1872-pattern had a 4-inch patch on either side and piping on the top and bottom; the rest of the collar was of dark blue to match the coat). Gold lace chevrons were authorized for non-commissioned officers in 1884, as Bowen wears. He also has the service chevrons of bullion prescribed in 1884. (FSHM)

Below: The class of 1884 at the Artillery School of the U.S. Army, Fort Monroe, Virginia had spent two years at their assignment. All have the 1872-pattern officers' forage cap, some with the addition of the white cotton summer cover. All but the man standing front row fifth from the right wear the 1875-pattern officers' blouse. The singular exception is James H. Oliver, who was a U.S. Navy ensign who participated in the course. As such, he wears the proper undress uniform of his branch of service for the period, with a white hat cover. (RGB)

Left: The 1885 through 1902 light artillery enlisted dress uniform worn with M1884, M1887 or M1889 boots for mounted duty. Cords, plume, and all facings are scarlet. From 1872, trouser stripes were to be ½-inch for corporals and 1-inch for sergeants. (NA)

Above: Starting in 1884 the scarlet piping was discontinued from artillerymen's five-button blouses. All wear the blouse here, with the 1872-pattern forage cap and 1872-pattern crossed cannon insignia and the regimental number (Second U.S. Artillery) evident. The men standing on either side of the picture are trumpeters, as indicated by the double ½-inch leg stripes, a distinction that had been used unofficially for many years, and was finally sanctioned by general orders in 1883. (UK)

Right: In addition to being proficient with artillery pieces, some individuals, including this first sergeant of the Third Artillery, were skilled with small arms. The two target-like silver insignia with black centers on the collar of this 1884-pattern five button blouse are marksmanship buttons, while the bar and the cross suspended from a bar are marksmanship and sharpshooter pins respectively, all of the 1885 model. (JG)

Because the 1872-pattern stamped brass insignia had fragile wires soldered to the back, some soldiers, such as this artillery-man of Battery F, Second U.S. Artillery, in his 1872-pattern forage cap, attached the regimental number and battery letter to the crossed cannons to strengthen them. This image dates from *c.* 1885. (FAM)

Above: Taking time out to eat, these artillerymen (probably of Battery B, Third U.S. Artillery at Camp Sheridan, Illinois) wear a variety of issue clothing. Many are in the post-1884 blouse. Others have the 1883-pattern blue flannel pullover shirt. Those in white wear the stable frock, or in some cases the overalls that mounted troops were issued for stable duty, the first specification being printed in 1879. Suspenders (braces) were not issued until 1883, however, and even then were seldom seen exposed, this practice being against regulations. Nevertheless, off-white issue suspenders of the 1883-pattern are visible on the man standing in the background third from the left, over his 1883-pattern shirt. The man seated on the ground slightly in front of the tree has what seems to be civilian suspenders. (RGB)

Below: The white summer helmet had been provided on a trial basis at Fort Monroe, Virginia in 1877, and three years later was issued on a general basis to troops serving in hot climates. Here Battery A, Second U.S. Artillery, at Fort Riley, Kansas wear the 1880-pattern cork helmet covered in white drilling. All other items are garrison wear typical of the uniform for field artillerymen from 1885 until the early 20th century. (UK)

Left: Artillery batteries received a new type of guidon in 1886 that was to be made of scarlet banner silk with crossed cannon, regimental number, and battery letter applied on both sides in yellow silk. This is the guidon for Battery D, Fifth U.S. Artillery. (USCM)

Below: This image of a Second Artillery private shows the leggings that came onto the scene by the late 1880s. Mounted artillerymen often rode with metal stirrups rather than the wooden ones with leather covers used by cavalrymen. (UK)

Opposite page: Wearing a drab 1889-pattern campaign hat, 1886-pattern gauntlets, and the 1883-pattern dark blue shirt, this artillery private is ready for the field. His M1840 saber is suspended from the M1885 saber hanger that has been modified by having the brass hook bent upward. (FSHM)

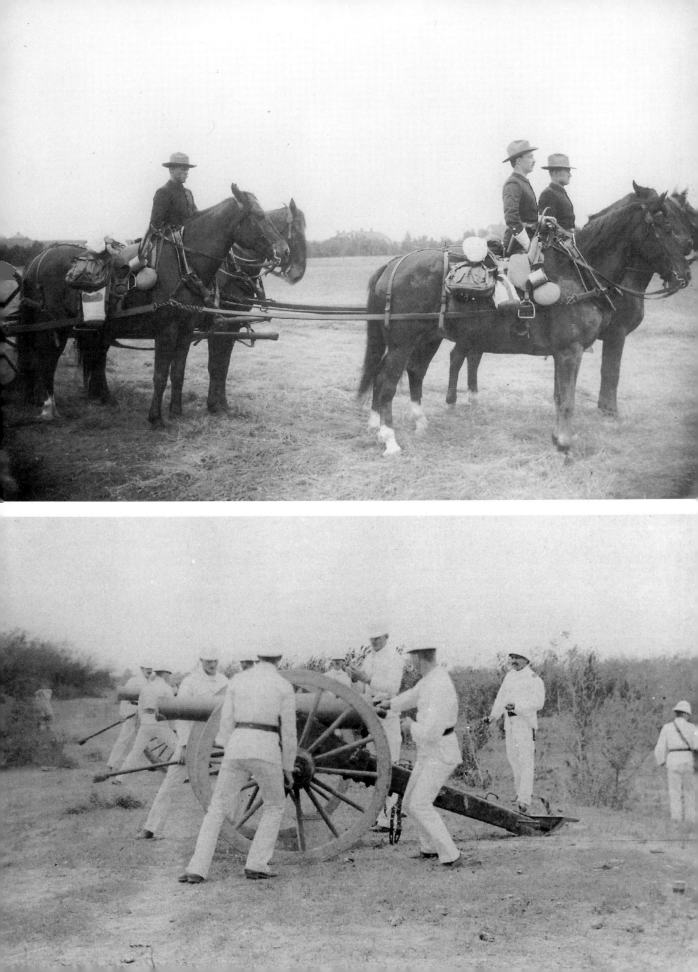

Opposite page, top: Ready to roll into action these horse artillerymen are uniformed in the field outfit of the 1889 through 1898 era, while the horses are equipped with nose bags, saddle bags, canteens, and canteen cups. Theoretically, these gunners were self-sufficient, even carrying revolvers in case they had to abandon their field pieces. (NA)

Opposite page, bottom: A half section of 3-inch ordnance rifles are put through their paces at Fort Brown, Texas in this 1893 photograph. The crew wears the 1880-pattern summer helmet, and the 1888- or 1889-pattern summer sack coat and trousers that had been prescribed for hot climates. The officer off to the side of the trail of the gun in the fore-ground has added shoulder straps with scarlet centers as appropriate rank to his blouse, despite the fact that regulations did not specify the combination of this garment with such insignia. (USAMHI)

Above: Lieutenant Knowelton of the Second Artillery was photographed in the 1895-pattern officers' field blouse which had a stand collar, hidden buttons, and black mohair trim. Shoulder straps were worn with this jacket, and a gold embroidered 'US' and crossed cannons were applied to the collar, with the regimental number in silver. Metallic collar insignia was also substituted in some instances. (UK)

Right: A private of Battery B, Second U.S. Artillery, appears in his barracks surrounded by light artillery uniform items of the 1895 through 1902 period, including the 1881-pattern dress helmet, the 1880-pattern summer helmet, the 1889-pattern campaign hat, and two 1895-pattern forage caps. These caps had a new one-piece crossed cannon insignia with a screw-back, and the battery number below and the regimental numeral above, both of which were fixed permanently to the device. (UK)

Below: This sergeant from Battery B, Third U.S. Artillery, wears the Heavy Artillery First Class Gunner's Badge that became available in 1897 to men who had scored 90% or better in a difficult examination in their field. There were four versions of this badge for specialists in communication, meteorology, full specialist (a combination of specialities) and first class gunner. (RGB)

Right: In 1898 a khaki jacket similar to the serge blouse, but with a stand collar and scarlet shoulder straps (loops) was prescribed for artillery officers, as worn by the captain on the far right of this photograph of Fort Riley's baseball team. His rank is indicated by two silver metal bars at the shoulder end of the loop, above which appears a gilt Arms of the United States, as per regulations. Further, the white cap cover on his 1895-pattern forage cap seems to have the ⅛-inch gold bullion cap cord rather than the white silk one called for in regulations. Second lieutenants through lieutenant colonels were supposed to have a 'US' in front of the branch insignia, although this captain does not. Colonels and general officers were to substitute the coat of arms on their collars and have the rank only on their loops. (UK)

Right: Lieutenant Colonel Rodney, Fourth U.S. Artillery, appears in the 1895-pattern officers' forage cap and the 1898 dark blue serge blouse with roll collar and four external pockets. This blouse used the same insignia combination (shoulder straps, US on collar, and crossed cannon) as the 1895-pattern sack coat with stand collar. In this instance, the officer has attached metal insignia to the collar rather than embroidered insignia. (UK)

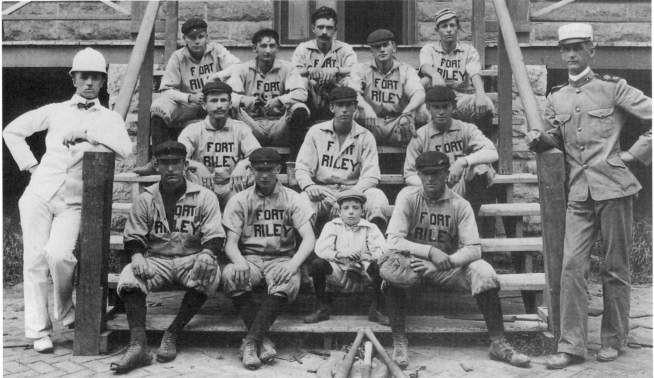

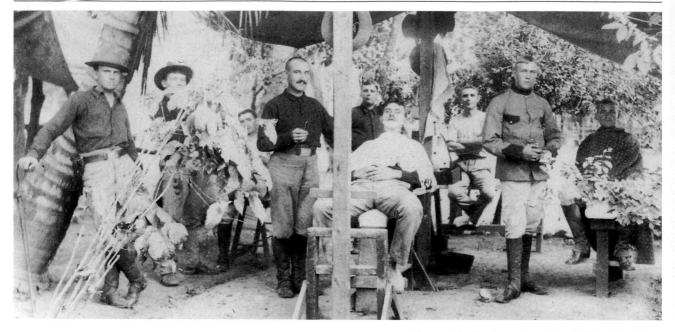

Above: The first version of the 1898 enlisted khaki blouse had scarlet cuffs, collar, and shoulder loops, as the private standing to the left of the man in the shaving chair illustrates. These men of Battery M, Seventh U.S. Artillery, one of the new units formed in preparation for possible war with Spain, also exhibit the combination of 1883-pattern blue wool shirts with both blue kersey trousers and khaki trousers. (RGB)

Left: Sergeant Max Muller strikes a pose in the next version of the khaki enlisted uniform which, by late in the Spanish-American War, had detachable shoulder loops in branch color, a plain stand collar, and cuffs without branch color. His headgear is the 1890-pattern white summer helmet which had a slightly different shape, including a longer rear, than the previous model. The sword belt is a company grade officer's dress belt, and seems to be a prop, as does the saber which is evidently a European style rather than American. (FSHM)

Opposite page: Private Charles Long, Battery F, Third U.S. Artillery, has strapped on the short-barrel 'Artillery' Colt revolver, and added the forage cap insignia to the upturned brim of his 1887-pattern campaign hat. Wearing his 1883-pattern field shirt and mounted reinforced 1885-pattern trousers, he is the image of a typical light artilleryman of the Spanish-American War. (UK)

Left: Sergeant Barnhardt, Battery O, Seventh U.S. Artillery, wears his campaign hat, which may be the 1899-pattern with large screen vents on the side of the crown, and scarlet worsted cords with acorn tips. The forage cap insignia was a personal addition. He wears what is probably the 1889-pattern enlisted overcoat with scarlet-lined cap thrown back to add dash. Chevrons were worn below the elbow on these coats so that they could be seen when the cape was down, thereby making it possible to distinguish the wearer's rank. (UK)

Above: Grimes' Battery, in the old blue wool shirt and light blue trousers, goes into action during the advance on Santiago de Cuba, during the Spanish-American War. (NA)

Below: A field piece from Cameron's Battery blasts away at the Spanish on 10 July 1898 during the Santiago fight. (NA)

Above: U.S. Artillerymen raft across a river near San Fabian, Philippine Islands, with a 3.2-inch gun during the Philippine Insurrection, in 1899. (NA)

Below: From 1899, lightning bolts were worn on the 1895-pattern forage cap for electrician sergeants of the coast artillery. The chevrons of these specialists also bore white embroidered lightning bolts above scarlet stripes that were outlined in white rather than the black chain stitching used for all other artillery NCOs. (NPS)

INDEX